The Pirates of Penzance

The Pirates of Penzance

Arthur Sullivan and W.S. Gilbert

The Pirates of Penzance was first published in 1879.

This edition published by Mint Editions 2021.

ISBN 9781513281445 | E-ISBN 9781513286464

Published by Mint Editions®

 MINT
EDITIONS

minteditionbooks.com

Publishing Director: Jennifer Newens
Design & Production: Rachel Lopez Metzger
Project Manager: Micaela Clark
Typesetting: Westchester Publishing Services

Dramatis Personæ

Major-General Stanley
The Pirate King
Samuel (his Lieutenant)
Frederic (the Pirate Apprentice)
Sergeant of Police
Mabel
Edith (General Stanley's Daughters)
Kate
Isabel
Ruth (a Pirate Maid of all Work)

Chorus of Pirates, Police, and General Stanley's Daughters.

Act I
A rocky sea-shore on the coast of Cornwall

Act II
A ruined chapel by moonlight

Act I

Scene.—*A rocky seashore on the coast of Cornwall. In the distance is a calm sea, on which a schooner is lying at anchor. As the curtain rises groups of pirates are discovered—some drinking, some playing cards.* Samuel, *the Pirate Lieutenant, is going from one group to another, filling the cups from a flask.* Frederic *is seated in a despondent attitude at the back of the scene.*

Opening Chorus.

All: Pour, oh, pour the pirate sherry;
  Fill, O fill the pirate glass;
 And, to make us more than merry,
  Let the pirate bumper pass.
Sam.: For today our pirate 'prentice
  Rises from indenture freed;
 Strong his arm, and keen his scent is
  He's a pirate now indeed!
All: Here's good luck to Frederic's ventures!
  Frederic's out of his indentures.
Sam.: Two and twenty, now he's rising,
  And alone he's fit to fly,
  Which we're bent on signalizing
  With unusual revelry.
All: Here's good luck to Frederic's ventures!
  Frederic's out of his indentures.
  Pour, O pour the pirate sherry, etc.

Frederic *rises and comes forward with* Pirate King, *who enters.*

King: Yes, Frederic, from to-day you rank as a full-blown member of our band.

All: Hurrah!

Fred.: My friends, I thank you all, from my heart, for your kindly wishes. Would that I could repay them as they deserve!

King: What do you mean?

Fred.: To-day I am out of my indentures, and to-day I leave you for ever.

King: But this is quite unaccountable; a keener hand at scuttling a Cunarder or cutting out a P. & O. never shipped a handspike.

FRED.: Yes, I have done my best for you. And why? It was my duty under my indentures, and I am the slave of duty. As a child I was regularly apprenticed to your band. It was through an error—no matter, the mistake was ours, not yours, and I was in honour bound by it.

SAM.: An error? What error?

FRED.: I may not tell you; it would reflect upon my well-loved Ruth.

RUTH *rises and comes forward.*

RUTH: Nay, dear master, my mind has long been gnawed by the cankering tooth of mystery. Better have it out at once.

SONG—RUTH.

RUTH: When Frederic was a little lad he proved so brave and daring,
His father thought he'd 'prentice him to some career seafaring.
I was, alas! his nurserymaid, and so it fell to my lot
To take and bind the promising boy apprentice to a pilot—
A LIFE not bad for a hardy lad, though surely not a high lot,
Though I'm a nurse, you might do worse than make your boy a pilot.

I was a stupid nursery maid, on breakers always steering,
And I did not catch the word aright, through being hard of hearing;
Mistaking my instructions, which within my brain did gyrate,
I took and bound this promising boy apprentice to a pirate.
A sad mistake it was to make and doom him to a vile lot.
I bound him to a pirate—you—instead of to a pilot.
I soon found out, beyond all doubt, the scope of this disaster,
But I hadn't the face to return to my place, and break it to my master.
A nurserymaid is not afraid of what you people call work,
So I made up my mind to go as a kind of piratical maid-of-all-work.
And that is how you find me now, a member of your shy lot,
Which you wouldn't have found, had he been bound apprentice to a pilot.

RUTH: Oh, pardon! Frederic, pardon! (*kneels*)

FRED.: Rise, sweet one, I have long pardoned you.

RUTH: (*rises*) The two words were so much alike!

FRED.: They were. They still are, though years have rolled over their heads. But this afternoon my obligation ceases. Individually, I love you all with affection unspeakable; but, collectively, I look upon you with a disgust that amounts to absolute detestation. Oh! pity me, my beloved friends, for such is my sense of duty that, once out of my indentures, I shall feel myself bound to devote myself heart and soul to your extermination!

ALL: Poor lad—poor lad! (*All weep*)

KING: Well, Frederic, if you conscientiously feel that it is your duty to destroy us, we cannot blame you for acting on that conviction. Always act in accordance with the dictates of your conscience, my boy, and chance the consequences.

SAM.: Besides, we can offer you but little temptation to remain with us. We don't seem to make piracy pay. I'm sure I don't know why, but we don't.

FRED.: I know why, but, alas! I mustn't tell you; it wouldn't be right.

KING: Why not, my boy? It's only half-past eleven, and you are one of us until the clock strikes twelve.

SAM.: True, and until then you are bound to protect our interests.

ALL: Hear, hear!

FRED.: Well, then, it is my duty, as a pirate, to tell you that you are too tender-hearted. For instance, you make a point of never attacking a weaker party than yourselves, and when you attack a stronger party you invariably get thrashed.

KING: There is some truth in that.

FRED.: Then, again, you make a point of never molesting an orphan!

SAM.: Of course: we are orphans ourselves, and know what it is.

FRED.: Yes, but it has got about, and what is the consequence? Every one we capture says he's an orphan. The last three ships we took proved to be manned entirely by orphans, and so we had to let them go. One would think that Great Britain's mercantile navy was recruited solely from her orphan asylums—which we know is not the case.

SAM.: But, hang it all! you wouldn't have us absolutely merciless?

FRED.: There's my difficulty; until twelve o'clock I would, after twelve I wouldn't. Was ever a man placed in so delicate a situation?

RUTH: And Ruth, your own Ruth, whom you love so well, and who has won her middle-aged way into your boyish heart, what is to become of her?

KING: Oh, he will take you with him. (*Hands* RUTH *to* FREDERIC)

FRED.: Well, Ruth, I feel some difficulty about you. It is true that I admire you very much, but I have been constantly at sea since I was eight years old, and yours is the only woman's face I have seen during that time. I think it is a sweet face.

RUTH: It is—oh, it is!

FRED.: I say I think it is; that is my impression. But as I have never had an opportunity of comparing you with other women, it is just possible I may be mistaken.

KING: True.

FRED.: What a terrible thing it would be if I were to marry this innocent person, and then find out that she is, on the whole, plain!

KING: Oh, Ruth is very well, very well indeed.

SAM.: Yes, there are the remains of a fine woman about Ruth.

FRED.: Do you really think so?

SAM.: I do.

FRED.: Then I will not be so selfish as to take her from you. In justice to her, and in consideration for you, I will leave her behind. (*Hands* RUTH *to* KING)

KING: No, Frederic, this must not be. We are rough men, who lead a rough life, but we are not so utterly heartless as to deprive thee of thy love. I think I am right in saying that there is not one here who would rob thee of this inestimable treasure for all the world holds dear.

ALL: (*loudly*) Not one!

KING: No, I thought there wasn't. Keep thy love, Frederic, keep thy love. (*Hands her back to* FREDERIC)

FRED.: You're very good, I'm sure. (*Exit* RUTH)

KING: Well, it's the top of the tide, and we must be off. Farewell, Frederic. When your process of extermination begins, let our deaths be as swift and painless as you can conveniently make them.

FRED.: I will! By the love I have for you, I swear it! Would that you could render this extermination unnecessary by accompanying me back to civilization!

KING: No, Frederic, it cannot be. I don't think much of our profession, but, contrasted with respectability, it is comparatively honest. No, Frederic, I shall live and die a Pirate King.

ARTHUR SULLIVAN AND W.S. GILBERT

King: Oh, better far to live and die
  Under the brave black flag I fly,
  Than play a sanctimonious part,
  With a pirate head and a pirate heart.
  Away to the cheating world go you,
  Where pirates all are well-to-do;
  But I'll be true to the song I sing,
  And live and die a Pirate King.
    For I am a Pirate King!
    And it is, it is a glorious thing
    To be a Pirate King!
    For I am a Pirate King!
All: You are!
    Hurrah for the Pirate King!
King: And it is, it is a glorious thing
    To be a Pirate King.
All: It is!
    Hurrah for the Pirate King!
King: When I sally forth to seek my prey
  I help myself in a royal way.
  I sink a few more ships, it's true,
  Than a well-bred monarch ought to do;
  But many a king on a first-class throne,
  If he wants to call his crown his own,
  Must manage somehow to get through
  More dirty work than ever I do,
    For I am a Pirate King!
    And it is, it is a glorious thing
    To be a Pirate King!
    For I am a Pirate King!
All: You are!
    Hurrah for the Pirate King!
King: And it is, it is a glorious thing
    To be a Pirate King.
All: It is!
    Hurrah for the Pirate King!
Exeunt all except Frederic. *Enter* Ruth.

RUTH: Oh, take me with you! I cannot live if I am left behind.

FRED.: Ruth, I will be quite candid with you. You are very dear to me, as you know, but I must be circumspect. You see, you are considerably older than I. A lad of twenty-one usually looks for a wife of seventeen.

RUTH: A wife of seventeen! You will find me a wife of a thousand!

FRED.: No, but I shall find you a wife of forty-seven, and that is quite enough. Ruth, tell me candidly and without reserve: compared with other women—how are you?

RUTH: I will answer you truthfully, master—I have a slight cold, but otherwise I am quite well.

FRED.: I am sorry for your cold, but I was referring rather to your personal appearance. Compared with other women, are you beautiful?

RUTH: (*bashfully*) I have been told so, dear master.

FRED.: Ah, but lately?

RUTH: Oh, no; years and years ago.

FRED.: What do you think of yourself?

RUTH: It is a delicate question to answer, but I think I am a fine woman.

FRED.: That is your candid opinion?

RUTH: Yes, I should be deceiving you if I told you otherwise.

FRED.: Thank you, Ruth. I believe you, for I am sure you would not practice on my inexperience. I wish to do the right thing, and if—I say if—you are really a fine woman, your age shall be no obstacle to our union! (*Chorus of Girls heard in the distance*) Hark! Surely I hear voices! Who has ventured to approach our all but inaccessible lair? Can it be Custom House? No, it does not sound like Custom House.

RUTH: (*aside*) Confusion! it is the voices of young girls! If he should see them I am lost.

FRED.: (*looking off*) By all that's marvellous, a bevy of beautiful maidens!

RUTH: (*aside*) Lost! lost! lost!

FRED.: How lovely, how surpassingly lovely is the plainest of them! What grace—what delicacy—what refinement! And Ruth—Ruth told me she was beautiful!

Fred.: Oh, false one, you have deceived me!
Ruth: I have deceived you?
Fred.: Yes, deceived me! (*Denouncing her*)

Duet—Frederic and Ruth.

Fred.: You told me you were fair as gold!
Ruth: (*wildly*) And, master, am I not so?
Fred.: And now I see you're plain and old.
Ruth: I'm sure I'm not a jot so.
Fred.: Upon my innocence you play.
Ruth: I'm not the one to plot so.
Fred.: Your face is lined, your hair is grey.
Ruth: It's gradually got so.
Fred.: Faithless woman, to deceive me,
      I who trusted so!
Ruth: Master, master, do not leave me!
     Hear me, ere you go!
   My love without reflecting,
    Oh, do not be rejecting!
Take a maiden tender—her affection raw and green,
    At very highest rating,
    Has been accumulating
Summers seventeen—summers seventeen.

Ensemble.

Ruth.	Fred.
Don't, beloved master,	Yes, your former master
Crush me with disaster.	Saves you from disaster.
What is such a dower to the	Your love would be uncomfortably
dower I have here?	fervid, it is clear
My love unabating	If, as you are stating
Has been accumulating	It's been accumulating
Forty-seven year—forty-seven year!	Forty-seven year—forty-seven year!

At the end he renounces her, and she goes off in despair.

What shall I do? Before these gentle maidens
I dare not show in this alarming costume!
No, no, I must remain in close concealment
Until I can appear in decent clothing!
Hides in cave as they enter climbing over the rocks.

GIRLS: Climbing over rocky mountain,
Skipping rivulet and fountain,
Passing where the willows quiver
By the ever-rolling river,
    Swollen with the summer rain;
Threading long and leafy mazes
Dotted with unnumbered daisies,
Scaling rough and rugged passes,
Climb the hardy little lasses,
    Till the bright sea-shore they gain!

EDITH: Let us gaily tread the measure,
Make the most of fleeting leisure,
Hail it as a true ally,
Though it perish by-and-by.

GIRLS: Hail it as a true ally,
Though it perish by-and-by.

EDITH: Every moment brings a treasure
Of its own especial pleasure;
Though the moments quickly die,
Greet them gaily as they fly.

KATE: Far away from toil and care,
Revelling in fresh sea-air,
Here we live and reign alone
In a world that's all our own.
Here, in this our rocky den,
Far away from mortal men,
We'll be queens, and make decrees—
They may honour them who please.

ALL: Let us gaily tread the measure, etc.

KATE: What a picturesque spot! I wonder where
we are!

EDITH: And I wonder where Papa is. We have left him ever so far behind.

ISABEL: Oh, he will be here presently! Remember poor Papa is not as young as we are, and we came over a rather difficult country.

KATE: But how thoroughly delightful it is to be so entirely alone! Why, in all probability we are the first human beings who ever set foot on this enchanting spot.

ISABEL: Except the mermaids—it's the very place for mermaids.

KATE: Who are only human beings down to the waist!

EDITH: And who can't be said strictly to set foot anywhere. Tails they may, but feet they cannot.

KATE: But what shall we do until Papa and the servants arrive with the luncheon?

EDITH: We are quite alone, and the sea is as smooth as glass. Suppose we take off our shoes and stockings and paddle?

ALL: Yes, yes! The very thing!

They prepare to carry, out the suggestion. They have all taken off one shoe, when FREDERIC *comes forward from cave.*

FRED.: (*recitative*) Stop, ladies, pray!

GIRLS: (*Hopping on one foot*) A man!

FRED.: I had intended

> Not to intrude myself upon your notice
> In this effective but alarming costume;
> But under these peculiar circumstances,
> It is my bounden duty to inform you
> That your proceedings will not be unwitnessed!

EDITH: But who are you, sir? Speak! (*All hopping*)

FRED.: I am a pirate!

GIRLS: (*recoiling, hopping*) A pirate! Horror!

FRED.: Ladies, do not shun me!

> This evening I renounce my vile profession;
> And, to that end, O pure and peerless maidens!
> Oh, blushing buds of ever-blooming beauty!
> I, sore at heart, implore your kind assistance.

EDITH: How pitiful his tale!

KATE: How rare his beauty!

GIRLS: How pitiful his tale! How rare his beauty!

FRED.: Oh, is there not one maiden breast
  Which does not feel the moral beauty
 Of making worldly interest
  Subordinate to sense of duty?
 Who would not give up willingly
  All matrimonial ambition,
 To rescue such a one as I
  From his unfortunate position?
GIRLS: Alas! there's not one maiden breast
  Which seems to feel the moral beauty
 Of making worldly interest
  Subordinate to sense of duty!
FRED.: Oh, is there not one maiden here
  Whose homely face and bad complexion
 Have caused all hope to disappear
  Of ever winning man's affection?
 To such an one, if such there be,
  I swear by Heaven's arch above you,
 If you will cast your eyes on me,
  However plain you be—I'll love you!
GIRLS: Alas! there's not one maiden here
  Whose homely face and bad complexion
 Have caused all hope to disappear
  Of ever winning man's affection!
FRED.: (*in despair*) Not one?
GIRLS: No, no—not one!
FRED.: Not one?
GIRLS: No, no!
MABEL *enters.*
MABEL: Yes, one!
GIRLS: 'Tis Mabel!
MABEL: Yes, 'tis Mabel!

RECITATIVE—MABEL.

Oh, sisters, deaf to pity's name,
 For shame!

It's true that he has gone astray,
        But pray
Is that a reason good and true
        Why you
Should all be deaf to pity's name?
GIRLS: (*aside*) The question is, had he not been
        A thing of beauty,
Would she be swayed by quite as keen
        A sense of duty?
MABEL: For shame, for shame, for shame!

SONG—MABEL.

MABEL: Poor wandering one!
    Though thou hast surely strayed,
        Take heart of grace,
        Thy steps retrace,
    Poor wandering one!
    Poor wandering one!
    If such poor love as mine
        Can help thee find
        True peace of mind—
    Why, take it, it is thine!
        Take heart, fair days will shine;
        Take any heart—take mine!
GIRLS: Take heart; no danger lowers;
    Take any heart-but ours!
Exeunt MABEL *and* FREDERIC. EDITH *beckons her sisters, who form a semicircle around her.*
EDITH: What ought we to do,
        Gentle sisters, say?
    Propriety, we know,
        Says we ought to stay;
    While sympathy exclaims,
        "Free them from your tether—
    Play at other games—
        Leave them here together."
KATE: Her case may, any day,
        Be yours, my dear, or mine.

Let her make her hay
    While the sun doth shine.
Let us compromise
    (*Our hearts are not of leather*):
Let us shut our eyes,
    And talk about the weather.
GIRLS: Yes, yes, let's talk about the weather.

CHATTERING CHORUS.

How beautifully blue the sky,
The glass is rising very high,
Continue fine I hope it may,
And yet it rained but yesterday.
Tomorrow it may pour again
(*I hear the country wants some rain*),
Yet people say, I know not why,
That we shall have a warm July.
Enter MABEL *and* FREDERIC.
During MABEL'*s solo the Girls continue chatter pianissimo, but listening eagerly all the time.*

SOLO—MABEL.

Did ever maiden wake
    From dream of homely duty,
To find her daylight break
    With such exceeding beauty?
Did ever maiden close
    Her eyes on waking sadness,
To dream of such exceeding gladness?
FRED.: Ah, yes! ah, yes! this is exceeding gladness!
GIRLS: How beautifully blue the sky, etc.

SOLO—FREDERIC.

During this, Girls continue their chatter pianissimo as before, but listening intently all the time.

Did ever pirate roll
  His soul in guilty dreaming,
 And wake to find that soul
  With peace and virtue beaming?

ENSEMBLE.

MABEL.	FREDERIC.	GIRLS.
Did ever maiden wake,	Did ever pirate loathed,	How beautifully blue the sky, etc.
From dream of homely duty	Forsake his hideous mission	
To find her daylight break	To find himself betrothed	
With such exceeding beauty!	To lady of position!	

RECITATIVE—FREDERIC.

Stay, we must not lose our senses;
  Men who stick at no offences
   Will anon be here!
 Piracy their dreadful trade is;
  Pray you, get you hence, young ladies,
   While the coast is clear!

FREDERIC *and* MABEL *retire.*

GIRLS: No, we must not lose our senses,
  If they stick at no offences
   We should not be here!
 Piracy their dreadful trade is—
  Nice companions for young ladies!
   Let us disappear.

During this chorus the Pirates have entered stealthily, and formed in a semicircle behind the Girls. As the Girls move to go off, each Pirate seizes a Girl.

KING *seizes*

EDITH *and* ISABEL, SAMUEL *seizes* KATE.

GIRLS: Too late!

PIRATES: Ha, ha!

GIRLS: Too late!

PIRATES: Ho, ho!
 Ha, ha, ha, ha! Ho, ho, ho, ho!

(Pirates pass in front of Girls)
PIRATES.
Here's a first-rate opportunity
To get married with impunity,
And indulge in the felicity
Of unbounded domesticity.
You shall quickly be parsonified,
Conjugally matrimonified,
By a doctor of divinity,
Who resides in this vicinity.
ALL: By a doctor of divinity
     Who resides in this vicinity,
     By a doctor, a doctor, a doctor,
     Of divinity, of divinity.

(Girls pass in front of Pirates)
GIRLS.
We have missed our opportunity
Of escaping with impunity;
So farewell to the felicity
Of our maiden domesticity!
We shall quickly be parsonified,
Conjugally matrimonified,
By a doctor of divinity,
Who resides in this vicinity.

RECITATIVE—MABEL *(coming forward)*.

Hold, monsters! Ere your pirate caravanserai
     Proceed, against our will, to wed us all,
Just bear in mind that we are Wards in Chancery,
     And father is a Major-General!
SAM.: *(cowed)* We'd better pause, or danger may befall,
     Their father is a Major-General.
GIRLS: Yes, yes; he is a Major-General!
The MAJOR-GENERAL *has entered unnoticed, on rock.*
GEN.: Yes, yes, I am a Major-General!
SAM.: For he is a Major-General!
ALL: He is! Hurrah for the Major-General!
GEN.: And it is, it is a glorious thing
     To be a Major-General!
ALL: It is! Hurrah for the Major-General!

SONG—MAJOR-GENERAL.

GEN.: I am the very model of a modern Major-General,
     I've information vegetable, animal, and mineral,
     I know the kings of England, and I quote the fights historical
     From Marathon to Waterloo, in order categorical;

I'm very well acquainted, too, with matters mathematical,
I understand equations, both the simple and quadratical,
About binomial theorem I'm teeming with a lot o' news—
With many cheerful facts about the square of the hypotenuse.

ALL: With many cheerful facts, etc.

GEN.: I'm very good at integral and differential calculus;
I know the scientific names of beings animalculous:
In short, in matters vegetable, animal, and mineral,
I am the very model of a modern Major-General.

ALL: In short, in matters vegetable, animal, and mineral,
He is the very model of a modern Major-General.

GEN.: I know our mythic history, King Arthur's and Sir Caradoc's;
I answer hard acrostics, I've a pretty taste for paradox,
I quote in elegiacs all the crimes of Heliogabalus,
In conics I can floor peculiarities parabolous;
I can tell undoubted Raphaels from Gerard Dows and Zoffanies,
I know the croaking chorus from the Frogs of Aristophanes!
Then I can hum a fugue of which I've heard the music's din afore,
And whistle all the airs from that infernal nonsense Pinafore.

ALL: And whistle all the airs, etc.

GEN.: Then I can write a washing bill in Babylonic cuneiform,
And tell you every detail of Caractacus's uniform:
In short, in matters vegetable, animal, and mineral,
I am the very model of a modern Major-General.

ALL: In short, in matters vegetable, animal, and mineral,
He is the very model of a modern Major-General.

GEN.: In fact, when I know what is meant by "mamelon" and "ravelin",
When I can tell at sight a Mauser rifle from a javelin,
When such affairs as sorties and surprises I'm more wary at,
And when I know precisely what is meant by "commissariat",
When I have learnt what progress has been made in modern gunnery,
When I know more of tactics than a novice in a nunnery;
In short, when I've a smattering of elemental strategy,
You'll say a better Major-General has never sat a gee.

ALL: You'll say a better Major-General, etc.

GEN.: For my military knowledge, though I'm plucky and adventury,
Has only been brought down to the beginning of the century;
But still, in matters vegetable, animal, and mineral,
I am the very model of a modern Major-General.

ALL: But still, in matters vegetable, animal, and mineral,
     He is the very model of a modern Major-General.

GEN.: And now that I've introduced myself, I should like to have
     some idea of what's going on.

KATE: Oh, Papa—we—

SAM.: Permit me, I'll explain in two words: we propose to marry your
     daughters.

GEN.: Dear me!

GIRLS: Against our wills, Papa—against our wills!

GEN.: Oh, but you mustn't do that! May I ask—this is a
     picturesque uniform, but I'm not familiar with it. What are
     you?

KING: We are all single gentlemen.

GEN.: Yes, I gathered that—Anything else?

KING: No, nothing else.

EDITH: Papa, don't believe them; they are pirates—the famous Pirates
     of Penzance!

GEN.: The Pirates of Penzance! I have often heard of them.

MABEL: All except this gentleman—(*indicating* FREDERIC)—who
     was a pirate once, but who is out of his indentures to day, and who
     means to lead a blameless life evermore.

GEN.: But wait a bit. I object to pirates as sons-in-law.

KING: We object to Major-Generals as fathers-in-law. But we waive
     that point. We do not press it. We look over it.

GEN.: (*aside*) Hah! an idea! (*aloud*) And do you mean to say that you
     would deliberately rob me of these, the sole remaining props of
     my old age, and leave me to go through the remainder of my life
     unfriended, unprotected, and alone?

KING: Well, yes, that's the idea.

GEN.: Tell me, have you ever known what it is to be an orphan?

PIRATES: (*disgusted*) Oh, dash it all!

KING: Here we are again!

GEN.: I ask you, have you ever known what it is to be an orphan?

KING: Often!

GEN.: Yes, orphan. Have you ever known what it is to be one?

KING: I say, often.

ALL: (*disgusted*) Often, often, often. (*Turning away*)

GEN.: I don't think we quite understand one another. I ask you, have
     you ever known what it is to be an orphan, and you say "orphan".

As I understand you, you are merely repeating the word "orphan" to show that you understand me.

KING: I didn't repeat the word often.

GEN.: Pardon me, you did indeed.

KING: I only repeated it once.

GEN.: True, but you repeated it.

KING: But not often.

GEN.: Stop! I think I see where we are getting confused. When you said "orphan", did you mean "orphan"—a person who has lost his parents, or "often", frequently?

KING: Ah! I beg pardon—I see what you mean—frequently.

GEN.: Ah! you said "often", frequently.

KING: No, only once.

GEN.: (*irritated*) Exactly—you said "often", frequently, only once.

FINALE—ACT I.

GEN.: Oh, men of dark and dismal fate,
  Forgo your cruel employ,
 Have pity on my lonely state,
  I am an orphan boy!

KING AND SAM.: An orphan boy?

GEN.: An orphan boy!

PIRATES: How sad, an orphan boy.

GEN.: These children whom you see
  Are all that I can call my own!

PIRATES: Poor fellow!

GEN.: Take them away from me,
  And I shall be indeed alone.

PIRATES: Poor fellow!

GEN.: If pity you can feel,
  Leave me my sole remaining joy—
 See, at your feet they kneel;
 Your hearts you cannot steel
 Against the sad, sad tale of the lonely orphan boy!

PIRATES: (*sobbing*) Poor fellow!
  See at our feet they kneel;
  Our hearts we cannot steel
 Against the sad, sad tale of the lonely orphan boy!

KING AND SAM.: The orphan boy!
　　See at our feet they kneel, etc.

ENSEMBLE.

GENERAL. (*aside*)	GIRLS. (*aside*)	PIRATES. (*aside*)
I'm telling a terrible story	He is telling a terrible story	If he's telling a story
But it doesn't diminish my glory;	Which will tend to diminish his glory;	He shall die by a death that is gory,
For they would have taken my daughters	Though they would have taken his daughters	One of the cruellest slaughters
Over the billowy waters,	Over the billowy waters,	That ever were known in these waters;
If I hadn't, in elegant diction,	It is easy, in elegant diction,	It is easy, in elegant diction,
Indulged in an innocent fiction;	To call it an innocent fiction;	To call it an innocent fiction;
Which is not in the same category	But it comes in the same category	But it comes in the same category
As telling a regular terrible story.	As telling a regular terrible story.	As telling a regular terrible story.

KING: Although our dark career
　　Sometimes involves the crime of stealing,
　We rather think that we're
　　Not altogether void of feeling.
　Although we live by strife,
　　We're always sorry to begin it,
　For what, we ask, is life
　　Without a touch of Poetry in it?
ALL: (*kneeling*) Hail, Poetry, thou heav'n-born maid!
　　Thou gildest e'en the pirate's trade.
　Hail, flowing fount of sentiment!
　　All hail, divine emollient! (*All rise*)
KING: You may go, for you're at liberty, our pirate rules protect you,
　　And honorary members of our band we do elect you!
SAM.: For he is an orphan boy!
CHORUS: He is! Hurrah for the orphan boy!
GEN.: And it sometimes is a useful thing
　　To be an orphan boy.
CHORUS: It is! Hurrah for the orphan boy!

Oh, happy day, with joyous glee
We/They will away and married be!
Should it befall auspiciously,
Her/Our sisters all will bridesmaids be!

RUTH *enters and comes down to* FREDERIC.

RUTH: Oh, master, hear one word, I do implore you!
Remember Ruth, your Ruth, who kneels before you!
PIRATES: Yes, yes, remember Ruth, who kneels before you!
FRED.: Away, you did deceive me!
PIRATES: (*Threatening* RUTH) Away, you did deceive him!
RUTH: Oh, do not leave me!
PIRATES: Oh, do not leave her!
FRED.: Away, you grieve me!
PIRATES: Away, you grieve him!
FRED.: I wish you'd leave me! (FREDERIC *casts* RUTH *from him*)
PIRATES: We wish you'd leave him!

Ensemble.

Pray observe the magnanimity
They/We display to lace and dimity!
Never was such opportunity
To get married with impunity,
But they/we give up the felicity
Of unbounded domesticity,
Though a doctor of divinity
Resides in this vicinity

Girls and MAJOR-GENERAL *go up rocks, while* PIRATES *indulge in a wild dance of delight on stage. The* MAJOR-GENERAL *produces a British flag, and the* PIRATE KING, *produces a black flag with skull and crossbones. Enter* RUTH, *who makes a final appeal to* FREDERIC, *who casts her from him.*

END OF ACT I

Act II

SCENE.–*A ruined chapel by moonlight. Ruined Gothic windows at back.* MAJOR-GENERAL STANLEY *discovered seated pensively, surrounded by his daughters.*

CHORUS.

Oh, dry the glistening tear
 That dews that martial cheek;
Thy loving children hear,
 In them thy comfort seek.
With sympathetic care
 Their arms around thee creep,
For oh, they cannot bear
 To see their father weep!

Enter MABEL.

SOLO—MABEL.

Dear father, why leave your bed
 At this untimely hour,
When happy daylight is dead,
 And darksome dangers lower?
See, heaven has lit her lamp,
 The twilight hour is past,
And the chilly night air is damp,
 And the dews are falling fast!
Dear father, why leave your bed
 When happy daylight is dead?

CHORUS: Oh, dry the glistening tear, etc.

FREDERIC *enters.*

MABEL: Oh, Frederic, cannot you, in the calm excellence of your wisdom, reconcile it with your conscience to say something that will relieve my father's sorrow?

FRED.: I will try, dear Mabel. But why does he sit, night after night, in this draughty old ruin?

GEN.: Why do I sit here? To escape from the pirates' clutches, I described myself as an orphan; and, heaven help me, I am no orphan! I come here to humble myself before the tombs of my ancestors, and to implore their pardon for having brought dishonour on the family escutcheon.

FRED.: But you forget, sir, you only bought the property a year ago, and the stucco on your baronial castle is scarcely dry.

GEN.: Frederic, in this chapel are ancestors: you cannot deny that. With the estate, I bought the chapel and its contents. I don't know whose ancestors they were, but I know whose ancestors they are, and I shudder to think that their descendant by purchase (*if I may so describe myself*) should have brought disgrace upon what, I have no doubt, was an unstained escutcheon.

FRED.: Be comforted. Had you not acted as you did, these reckless men would assuredly have called in the nearest clergyman, and have married your large family on the spot.

GEN.: I thank you for your proffered solace, but it is unavailing. I assure you, Frederic, that such is the anguish and remorse I feel at the abominable falsehood by which I escaped these easily deluded pirates, that I would go to their simple-minded chief this very night and confess all, did I not fear that the consequences would be most disastrous to myself. At what time does your expedition march against these scoundrels?

FRED.: At eleven, and before midnight I hope to have atoned for my involuntary association with the pestilent scourges by sweeping them from the face of the earth—and then, dear Mabel, you will be mine!

GEN.: Are your devoted followers at hand?

FRED.: They are, they only wait my orders.

RECIT—GENERAL.

Then, Frederic, let your escort lion-hearted
Be summoned to receive a General's blessing,
Ere they depart upon their dread adventure.

FRED.: Dear, sir, they come.

Enter Police, marching in single file. They form in line, facing audience.

When the foeman bares his steel,
    Tarantara! tarantara!
We uncomfortable feel,
    Tarantara!
And we find the wisest thing,
    Tarantara! tarantara!
Is to slap our chests and sing,
    Tarantara!
For when threatened with emeutes,
    Tarantara! tarantara!
And your heart is in your boots,
    Tarantara!
There is nothing brings it round
Like the trumpet's martial sound,
Like the trumpet's martial sound
ALL: Tarantara! tarantara!, etc.
MABEL: Go, ye heroes, go to glory,
  Though you die in combat gory,
  Ye shall live in song and story.
    Go to immortality!
  Go to death, and go to slaughter;
  Die, and every Cornish daughter
  With her tears your grave shall water.
    Go, ye heroes, go and die!
GIRLS: Go, ye heroes, go and die!

Sergeant, with Police.

Though to us it's evident,
    Tarantara! tarantara!
These attentions are well meant,
    Tarantara!
Such expressions don't appear,
    Tarantara! tarantara!
Calculated men to cheer,
    Tarantara!
Who are going to meet their fate

In a highly nervous state.
    Tarantara! tarantara! tarantara!
Still to us it's evident
These attentions are well meant.
    Tarantara! tarantara! tarantara!
EDITH: Go and do your best endeavour,
    And before all links we sever,
    We will say farewell for ever.
    Go to glory and the grave!
GIRLS: Go to glory and the grave!
    For your foes are fierce and ruthless,
    False, unmerciful, and truthless;
    Young and tender, old and toothless,
    All in vain their mercy crave.
SERG.: We observe too great a stress,
    On the risks that on us press,
    And of reference a lack
    To our chance of coming back.
    Still, perhaps it would be wise
    Not to carp or criticise,
    For it's very evident
    These attentions are well meant.
POLICE: Yes, it's very evident
    These attentions are well meant, etc.

ENSEMBLE.

CHORUS OF ALL BUT POLICE.	CHORUS OF POLICE.
Go ye heroes, go to glory, etc.	When the foeman bears his steel, etc.

GEN.: Away, away!
POLICE: (*without moving*) Yes, yes, we go.
GEN.: These pirates slay.
POLICE: Tarantara!
GEN.: Then do not stay.
POLICE: Tarantara!
GEN.: Then why this delay?
POLICE: All right, we go.
    Yes, forward on the foe!
GEN.: Yes, but you don't go!

POLICE: We go, we go
  Yes, forward on the foe!
GEN.: Yes, but you don't go!
ALL: At last they really go!
Exeunt Police. MABEL *tears herself from* FREDERIC *and exit, followed by her sisters, consoling her. The* MAJOR-GENERAL *and others follow.* FREDERIC *remains alone.*

RECITATIVE—FREDERIC.

Now for the pirates' lair! Oh, joy unbounded!
Oh, sweet relief! Oh, rapture unexampled!
At last I may atone, in some slight measure,
For the repeated acts of theft and pillage
Which, at a sense of duty's stern dictation,
I, circumstance's victim, have been guilty!
PIRATE KING *and* RUTH *appear, armed.*
KING: Young Frederic! (*Covering him with pistol*)
FRED.: Who calls?
KING: Your late commander!
RUTH: And I, your little Ruth! (*Covering him with pistol*)
FRED.: Oh, mad intruders,
  How dare ye face me? Know ye not, oh rash ones,
  That I have doomed you to extermination?
KING *and* RUTH *hold a pistol to each ear.*
KING: Have mercy on us! hear us, ere you slaughter!
FRED.: I do not think I ought to listen to you.
  Yet, mercy should alloy our stern resentment,
  And so I will be merciful—say on!

TRIO—RUTH, KING, and FREDERIC.

RUTH: When you had left our pirate fold,
    We tried to raise our spirits faint,
  According to our custom old,
    With quip and quibble quaint.
  But all in vain the quips we heard,
    We lay and sobbed upon the rocks,
  Until to somebody occurred
    A startling paradox.

FRED.: A paradox?

RUTH: (*laughing*) A paradox!
  A most ingenious paradox!
  We've quips and quibbles heard in flocks,
  But none to beat this paradox!

ALL: A paradox, a paradox, etc.

KING: We knew your taste for curious quips,
    For cranks and contradictions queer;
  And with the laughter on our lips,
    We wished you there to hear.
  We said, "If we could tell it him,
    How Frederic would the joke enjoy!"
  And so we've risked both life and limb
    To tell it to our boy.

FRED.: (*interested*) That paradox?

KING: (*laughing*) That most ingenious paradox!
  We've quips and quibbles heard in flocks,
  But none to beat that paradox!

ALL: A paradox, a paradox, etc.

CHANT—KING.

For some ridiculous reason, to which, however, I've no desire to be disloyal, Some person in authority, I don't know who, very likely the Astronomer Royal, has decided that, although for such a beastly month as February, twenty-eight days as a rule are plenty.

One year in every four his days shall be reckoned as nine and twenty. Through some singular coincidence—I shouldn't be surprised if it were owing to the agency of an ill-natured fairy—You are the victim of this clumsy arrangement, having been born in leap-year, on the twenty-ninth of February.

And so, by a simple arithmetical process, you'll easily discover, that though you've lived twenty-one years, yet, if we go by birthdays, you're only five and a little bit over!

RUTH AND KING: Ha! ha! ha! ha!
  Ho! ho! ho! ho!

FRED.: Dear me!
  Let's see! (*counting on fingers*)
  Yes, yes; with yours my figures do agree!

ALL: Ha! ha! ha! ho! ho! ho! ho!

FRED.: (*more amused than any*) How quaint the ways of Paradox!
  At common sense she gaily mocks!
  Though counting in the usual way,
      Years twenty-one I've been alive,
  Yet, reckoning by my natal day,
      I am a little boy of five!

RUTH AND KING: He is a little boy of five! Ha! ha! ha!

ALL: A paradox, a paradox,
  A most ingenious paradox!
  Ha! ha! ha! ha! ha! ha! ha! ha!, etc.

RUTH *and* KING *throw themselves back on seats, exhausted with laughter.*

FRED.: Upon my word, this is most curious—most absurdly whimsical.
  Five-and-a-quarter! No one would think it to look at me!

RUTH: You are glad now, I'll be bound, that you spared us. You would
  never have forgiven yourself when you discovered that you had
  killed two of your comrades.

FRED.: My comrades?

KING: (*rises*) I'm afraid you don't appreciate the delicacy of your
  position: You were apprenticed to us—

FRED.: Until I reached my twenty-first year.

KING: No, until you reached your twenty-first birthday (*producing document*),
  and, going by birthdays, you are as yet only five-and-a-quarter.

FRED.: You don't mean to say you are going to hold me to that?

KING: No, we merely remind you of the fact, and leave the rest to your
  sense of duty.

RUTH: Your sense of duty!

FRED.: (*wildly*) Don't put it on that footing! As I was merciful to you
  just now, be merciful to me! I implore you not to insist on the letter
  of your bond just as the cup of happiness is at my lips!

RUTH: We insist on nothing; we content ourselves with pointing out
  to you your duty.

KING: Your duty!

FRED.: (*after a pause*) Well, you have appealed to my sense of duty, and
  my duty is only too clear. I abhor your infamous calling; I shudder
  at the thought that I have ever been mixed up with it; but duty is
  before all—at any price I will do my duty.

KING: Bravely spoken! Come, you are one of us once more.

FRED.: Lead on, I follow. (*suddenly*) Oh, horror!

RUTH AND KING: What is the matter?

FRED.: Ought I to tell you? No, no, I cannot do it; and yet, as one of your band—

KING: Speak out, I charge you by that sense of conscientiousness to which we have never yet appealed in vain.

FRED.: General Stanley, the father of my Mabel—

RUTH AND KING: Yes, yes!

FRED.: He escaped from you on the plea that he was an orphan?

KING: He did.

FRED.: It breaks my heart to betray the honoured father of the girl I adore, but as your apprentice I have no alternative. It is my duty to tell you that General Stanley is no orphan!

RUTH AND KING: What!

FRED.: More than that, he never was one!

KING: Am I to understand that, to save his contemptible life, he dared to practise on our credulous simplicity? (FREDERIC *nods as he weeps*) Our revenge shall be swift and terrible. We will go and collect our band and attack Tremorden Castle this very night.

FRED.: But stay—

KING: Not a word! He is doomed!

TRIO.

KING and RUTH.
Away, away! my heart's on fire;
I burn, this base deception to repay.
This very night my vengeance dire

Shall glut itself in gore. Away,
    away!
KING: With falsehood foul
    He tricked us of our brides.
        Let vengeance howl;
    The Pirate so decides.
        Our nature stern
    He softened with his lies,
        And, in return,
    Tonight the traitor dies.
ALL: Yes, yes! tonight the traitor dies!

FREDERIC.
Away, away! ere I expire—
I find my duty hard to do today!
My heart is filled with anguish
    dire,
It strikes me to the core. Away,
    away!

RUTH: Tonight he dies!
KING: Yes, or early tomorrow.
FRED.: His girls likewise?
RUTH: They will welter in sorrow.
KING: The one soft spot—
RUTH: In their natures they cherish—
FRED.: And all who plot—
KING: To abuse it shall perish!
ALL: Tonight he dies, etc.
Exeunt KING *and* RUTH. *Enter* MABEL.

RECITATIVE.—MABEL.

All is prepared, your gallant crew await you.
My Frederic in tears? It cannot be
That lion-heart quails at the coming conflict?
FRED.: No, Mabel, no. A terrible disclosure
Has just been made. Mabel, my dearly-loved one,
I bound myself to serve the pirate captain
Until I reached my one-and-twentieth birthday—
MABEL: But you are twenty-one?
FRED.: I've just discovered
That I was born in leap-year, and that birthday
Will not be reached by me till nineteen forty!
MABEL: Oh, horrible! catastrophe appalling!
FRED.: And so, farewell!
MABEL: No, no! Ah, Frederic, hear me.

DUET.—MABEL and FREDERIC.

MABEL: Stay, Frederic, stay!
    They have no legal claim,
    No shadow of a shame
    Will fall upon thy name.
  Stay, Frederic, stay!
FRED.: Nay, Mabel, nay!
    Tonight I quit these walls,
    The thought my soul appalls,
    But when stern Duty calls,
  I must obey.

Ah, leave me not to pine
    Alone and desolate;
No fate seemed fair as mine,
    No happiness so great!
And Nature, day by day,
    Has sung in accents clear
This joyous roundelay,
      "He loves thee—he is here.
    Fa-la, la-la, Fa-la, la-la".
Fred.: Ah, must I leave thee here
    In endless night to dream,
Where joy is dark and drear,
    And sorrow all supreme—
Where nature, day by day,
    Will sing, in altered tone,
This weary roundelay,
      "He loves thee—he is gone.
    Fa-la, la-la, Fa-la, la-la."
Fred.: In 1940 I of age shall be,
    I'll then return, and claim you—I declare it!
Mabel: It seems so long!
Fred.: Swear that, till then, you will be true to me.
Mabel: Yes, I'll be strong!
    By all the Stanleys dead and gone, I swear it!

Ensemble.

    Oh, here is love, and here is truth,
      And here is food for joyous laughter:
    He/She will be faithful to his/her sooth
      Till we are wed, and even after.
Frederic *rushes to window and leaps out.*
Mabel: (*almost fainting*) No, I'll be brave! Oh, family descent,
    How great thy charm, thy sway how excellent!
    Come one and all, undaunted men in blue,
    A crisis, now, affairs are coming to!
Enter Police, marching in single file.

SERG.: Though in body and in mind,

POLICE: Tarantara! tarantara!

SERG.: We are timidly inclined,

POLICE: Tarantara!

SERG.: And anything but blind—

POLICE: Tarantara! tarantara!

SERG.: To the danger that's behind.

POLICE: Tarantara!

SERG.: Yet, when the danger's near,

POLICE: Tarantara! tarantara!

SERG.: We manage to appear—

POLICE: Tarantara!

SERG.: As insensible to fear
As anybody here.

POLICE: Tarantara! tarantara!, etc.

MABEL: Sergeant, approach! Young Frederic was to have led you to death and glory.

POLICE: That is not a pleasant way of putting it.

MABEL: No matter; he will not so lead you, for he has allied himself once more with his old associates.

POLICE: He has acted shamefully!

MABEL: You speak falsely. You know nothing about it. He has acted nobly.

POLICE: He has acted nobly!

MABEL: Dearly as I loved him before, his heroic sacrifice to his sense of duty has endeared him to me tenfold. He has done his duty. I will do mine. Go ye and do yours.

Exit MABEL.

POLICE: Right oh!

SERG.: This is perplexing.

POLICE: We cannot understand it at all.

SERG.: Still, as he is actuated by a sense of duty—

POLICE: That makes a difference, of course. At the same time, we repeat, we cannot understand it at all.

SERG.: No matter. Our course is clear: we must do our best to capture these pirates alone. It is most distressing to us to be the agents whereby our erring fellow-creatures are deprived of that liberty which is so dear to us all—but we should have thought of that before we joined the force.

POLICE: We should!
SERG.: It is too late now!
POLICE: It is!

SONG—SERGEANT.

SERG.: When a felon's not engaged in his employment—
POLICE: His employment,
SERG.: Or maturing his felonious little plans—
POLICE: Little plans,
SERG.: His capacity for innocent enjoyment—
POLICE: 'Cent enjoyment.
SERG.: Is just as great as any honest man's—
POLICE: Honest man's.
SERG.: Our feelings we with difficulty smother—
POLICE: 'Culty smother.
SERG.: When constabulary duty's to be done—
POLICE: To be done.
SERG.: Ah, take one consideration with another—
POLICE: With another,
SERG.: A policeman's lot is not a happy one.
POLICE: Ah, when constabulary duty's to be done, to be done,
    A policeman's lot is not a happy one, happy one.
SERG.: When the enterprising burglar's not a-burgling—
POLICE: Not a-burgling.
SERG.: When the cut-throat isn't occupied in crime—
POLICE: 'Pied in crime,
SERG.: He loves to hear the little brook a-gurgling—
POLICE: Brook a-gurgling,
SERG.: And listen to the merry village chime—
POLICE: Village chime.
SERG.: When the coster's finished jumping on his mother—
POLICE: On his mother,
SERG.: He loves to lie a-basking in the sun—
POLICE: In the sun.
SERG.: Ah, take one consideration with another—
POLICE: With another,
SERG.: A policeman's lot is not a happy one.
POLICE: Ah, when constabulary duty's to be done, to be done,

A policeman's lot is not a happy one, happy one.
Chorus of Pirates without, in the distance.

A rollicking band of pirates we,
Who, tired of tossing on the sea,
Are trying their hand at a burglaree,
With weapons grim and gory.

SERG.: Hush, hush! I hear them on the manor poaching,
With stealthy step the pirates are approaching.
Chorus of Pirates, resumed nearer.

We are not coming for plate or gold—
A story General Stanley's told—
We seek a penalty fifty-fold,
For General Stanley's story.

POLICE: They seek a penalty
PIRATES: Fifty-fold!

We seek a penalty
POLICE: Fifty-fold!
ALL: They/We seek a penalty fifty-fold,
For General Stanley's story.

SERG.: They come in force, with stealthy stride,
Our obvious course is now—to hide.

Police conceal themselves. As they do so, the Pirates are seen appearing at ruined windows. They enter cautiously, and come down stage. SAMUEL *is laden with burglarious tools and pistols, etc.*

CHORUS—PIRATES (*very loud*).

With cat-like tread,
Upon our prey we steal;
In silence dread,
Our cautious way we feel.
No sound at all,
We never speak a word,
A fly's foot-fall
Would be distinctly heard—

POLICE: (*pianissimo*) Tarantara, tarantara!
PIRATES: So stealthily the pirate creeps,
While all the household soundly sleeps.
Come, friends, who plough the sea,

        Truce to navigation;
        Take another station;
    Let's vary piracee
    With a little burglaree!
POLICE: (*pianissimo*) Tarantara, tarantara!
SAM.: (*distributing implements to various members of the gang*)
    Here's your crowbar and your centrebit,
    Your life-preserver—you may want to hit!
    Your silent matches, your dark lantern seize,
    Take your file and your skeletonic keys.
Enter KING, FREDERIC *and* RUTH.
PIRATES: (*fortissimo*) With cat-like tread, etc.
POLICE: (*pianissimo*) Tarantara! tarantara!

RECITATIVE.

FRED.: Hush, hush! not a word; I see a light inside!
    The Major-General comes, so quickly hide!
PIRATES: Yes, yes, the Major-General comes!
Pirates conceal themselves. Exeunt KING, FREDERIC, SAMUEL, *and* RUTH.
POLICE: Yes, yes, the Major-General comes!
GEN.: (*entering in dressing-gown, carrying a light*)
    Yes, yes, the Major-General comes!

SOLO—GENERAL.

Tormented with the anguish dread
    Of falsehood unatoned,
I lay upon my sleepless bed,
    And tossed and turned and groaned.
The man who finds his conscience ache
    No peace at all enjoys;
And as I lay in bed awake,
    I thought I heard a noise.
MEN: He thought he heard a noise—ha! ha!
GEN.: No, all is still
    In dale, on hill;
My mind is set at ease—
    So still the scene,

It must have been
The sighing of the breeze.

BALLAD—GENERAL.

Sighing softly to the river
    Comes the loving breeze,
Setting nature all a-quiver,
    Rustling through the trees.
MEN: Through the trees.
GEN.: And the brook, in rippling measure,
    Laughs for very love,
While the poplars, in their pleasure,
    Wave their arms above.
MEN: Yes, the trees, for very love,
    Wave their leafy arms above.
      River, river, little river,
    May thy loving prosper ever!
    Heaven speed thee, poplar tree,
    May thy wooing happy be.
GEN.: Yet, the breeze is but a rover,
    When he wings away,
Brook and poplar mourn a lover
    Sighing, "Well-a-day!"
MEN: Well-a-day!
GEN.: Ah! the doing and undoing,
    That the rogue could tell!
When the breeze is out a-wooing,
    Who can woo so well?
MEN: Shocking tales the rogue could tell,
    Nobody can woo so well.
      Pretty brook, thy dream is over,
    For thy love is but a rover;
    Sad the lot of poplar trees,
    Courted by a fickle breeze!

Enter the GENERAL'*s daughters, led by* MABEL, *all in white peignoirs and night-caps, and carrying lighted candles.*
GIRLS: Now what is this, and what is that, and why does father leave
    his rest

At such a time of night as this, so very incompletely dressed?
Dear father is, and always was, the most methodical of men!
It's his invariable rule to go to bed at half-past ten.
What strange occurrence can it be that calls dear father from his rest
At such a time of night as this, so very incompletely dressed?

Enter KING, SAMUEL, *and* FREDERIC.

KING: Forward, my men, and seize that General there!

They seize the GENERAL.

GIRLS: The pirates! the pirates! Oh, despair!

PIRATES: (*springing up*) Yes, we're the pirates, so despair!

GEN.: Frederic here! Oh, joy! Oh. rapture!
Summon your men and effect their capture!

MABEL: Frederic, save us!

FRED.: Beautiful Mabel,
I would if I could, but I am not able.

PIRATES: He's telling the truth, he is not able.

KING: With base deceit
You worked upon our feelings!
Revenge is sweet,
And flavours all our dealings!
With courage rare
And resolution manly,
For death prepare,
Unhappy General Stanley.

MABEL: (*wildly*) Is he to die, unshriven—unannealed?

GIRLS: Oh, spare him!

MABEL: Will no one in his cause a weapon wield?

GIRLS: Oh, spare him!

POLICE: (*springing up*) Yes, we are here, though hitherto concealed!

GIRLS: Oh, rapture!

POLICE: So to Constabulary, pirates yield!

GIRLS: Oh, rapture!

A struggle ensues between Pirates and Police, Eventually the Police are overcome and fall prostrate, the Pirates standing over them with drawn swords.

CHORUS OF PIRATES AND POLICE.

We/You triumph now, for well we trow
Your/Our mortal career's cut short;

No pirate band will take its stand
>   At the Central Criminal Court.
SERG.: To gain a brief advantage you've contrived,
>   But your proud triumph will not be long-lived.
KING: Don't say you are orphans, for we know that game.
SERG.: On your allegiance we've a stronger claim—
>   We charge you yield, we charge you yield,
>   In Queen Victoria's name!
KING: (*baffled*) You do?
POLICE: We do!
>   We charge you yield,
>   In Queen Victoria's name!
Pirates kneel, Police stand over them triumphantly.
KING: We yield at once, with humbled mien,
>   Because, with all our faults, we love our Queen.
POLICE: Yes, yes, with all their faults, they love their Queen.
ALL: Yes, yes, with all their faults, they love their Queen.
Police, holding Pirates by the collar, take out handkerchiefs and weep.
GEN.: Away with them, and place them at the bar!
Enter RUTH.
RUTH: One moment! let me tell you who they are.
>   They are no members of the common throng;
>   They are all noblemen who have gone wrong.
ALL: They are all noblemen who have gone wrong.
GEN.: No Englishman unmoved that statement hears,
>   Because, with all our faults, we love our House of Peers.
>   I pray you, pardon me, ex-Pirate King!
>   Peers will be peers, and youth will have its fling.
>   Resume your ranks and legislative duties,
>   And take my daughters, all of whom are beauties.

FINALE.

Poor wandering ones!
>   Though ye have surely strayed,
>   Take heart of grace,
>   Your steps retrace,
Poor wandering ones!
Poor wandering ones!

If such poor love as ours
Can help you find
True peace of mind,
Why, take it, it is yours!
ALL: Poor wandering ones! etc.

END OF OPERA

A Note About the Authors

Arthur Sullivan (1842–1900) and W.S. Gilbert (1836–1911) were theatrical collaborators during the nineteenth century. Prior to their partnership, Gilbert wrote and illustrated stories as a child, eventually developing his signature "topsy-turvy" style. Sullivan was raised in a musical family where he learned to play multiple instruments at an early age. Together, their talents would help produce a successful series of comic operas. Some notable titles include *The Pirates of Penzance*, *The Sorcerer*, *H.M.S. Pinafore*, and *The Mikado*.

A Note from the Publisher

Spanning many genres, from non-fiction essays to literature classics to children's books and lyric poetry, Mint Edition books showcase the master works of our time in a modern new package. The text is freshly typeset, is clean and easy to read, and features a new note about the author in each volume. Many books also include exclusive new introductory material. Every book boasts a striking new cover, which makes it as appropriate for collecting as it is for gift giving. Mint Edition books are only printed when a reader orders them, so natural resources are not wasted. We're proud that our books are never manufactured in excess and exist only in the exact quantity they need to be read and enjoyed. To learn more and view our library, go to minteditionbooks.com

bookfinity & MINT EDITIONS

Enjoy more of your favorite classics with Bookfinity,
a new search and discovery experience for readers.
With Bookfinity, you can discover more vintage
literature for your collection, find your Reader Type,
track books you've read or want to read,
and add reviews to your favorite books.
Visit www.bookfinity.com, and click on
Take the Quiz to get started.

Don't forget to follow us
@bookfinityofficial and @mint_editions